T0107460

# Love & Other Tragedies

*A collection of poems written by Julia Norris*

JULIA NORRIS

iUniverse, Inc.
Bloomington

**Love & Other Tragedies**
**A collection of poems written by Julia Norris**

Copyright © 2012 by Julia Norris.

All rights reserved. No part of this book may be used or reproduced by any means, graphic, electronic, or mechanical, including photocopying, recording, taping or by any information storage retrieval system without the written permission of the publisher except in the case of brief quotations embodied in critical articles and reviews.

iUniverse books may be ordered through booksellers or by contacting:

iUniverse
1663 Liberty Drive
Bloomington, IN 47403
www.iuniverse.com
1-800-Authors (1-800-288-4677)

Because of the dynamic nature of the Internet, any web addresses or links contained in this book may have changed since publication and may no longer be valid. The views expressed in this work are solely those of the author and do not necessarily reflect the views of the publisher, and the publisher hereby disclaims any responsibility for them.

Any people depicted in stock imagery provided by Thinkstock are models, and such images are being used for illustrative purposes only.
Certain stock imagery © Thinkstock.

ISBN: 978-1-4697-9820-2 (sc)
ISBN: 978-1-4697-9821-9 (ebk)

Printed in the United States of America

iUniverse rev. date: 03/05/2012

# Contents

## Life

## Loss

## Love

# Fight

When times are tough
And life is rough
When good times roll out
And bad times run in
Fight through today
Tomorrow will be a better day

When the thunder is sounding
And the rain is pounding
The path you're walking
Don't stop
Dance in the rain
Fight through the pain

When your heart is breaking
And your knees are shaking
Take a deep breath
And don't forget
To fight through the tears
Fight through your fears

In your darkest night
Do what is right
Fight
Fight to hold on
Hold on to your dreams
When life is beating you down
Don't frown
Fight back
Rise up
It's the ONLY way
You have to make
Your better days

# Rebel Child

*Born a rebel child*
*And I'll die the same*
*Try to push me*
*And I'll push the other way*
*Yeah I'm stubborn*
*And I'm proud*
*But*
*I was born a rebel child*
*And I'll die the same*
*No I won't follow you*
*But you can follow me*
*Cause I was born a rebel child*
*And I'll die the same*
*Try to change me*
*And I'll push you away*
*I was born a rebel child*
*And I'll die the same*

*~Julia Norris~*

# Just Me

They laugh about
The way I talk
The way I walk
How I dress
And how I'm just a mess
Judging glares
Hateful stares
As I walk by
Don't lie
I know you hate me
It ain't that hard to see
But hey
I'm only guilty of being me
And I don't have the time
To listen to your lies
I can see it in your eyes
If you don't like me
Stay away
But if you do
That's cool too
Either way
Don't matter to me
You be you
And I'll be me
Cause all I can be
All I'm gonna be
Is just plain old me

# Anger

*Lying in my bed*
*Seeing red*
*Tears of hate*
*Roll down my face*
*Rage consumes me*
*Anger controls me*
*Years of pent-up pain*
*Driving me insane*
*I hear my screams*
*But it doesn't sound like me*
*Sweat pours down*
*Finally*
*My sanity is found*
*All that remains*
*Is the pain*
*Of losing control*

*~Julia Norris~*

# Get Away

Tired of expectation
Need a vacation
To get away
Why don't you say
Something other
Than everyone else is better
It's getting real old
Being told
To be more like someone
Other than me
Can't wait till I'm eighteen
Then I can leave
And go where I belong
Just a little longer
And I'll be gone
Until then,
I'll drown out your screams
And replace them with my dreams

# Words

Words
Break your heart
Words
Confuse your mind
Words
Simple letters
Words
Make you cry
Make you laugh
Words
Heals hearts
Words
Start wars
Words
So small
Yet so destructive

*~Julia Norris~*

# Change

Change
It's inevitable
Change
Always there
Sometimes good
Sometimes bad
Occasionally necessary
Change
Never ending
Change
Without warning
Change
Our biggest fear
Change
LIFE IS CHANGE

# High School

High school is
Judgmental stares
And hateful glares
Finding where you belong
Falling in—
And out of love
Rumors heard
Under lunchroom tables
Being labeled
High school is
Trial and error
Make-ups and break-ups
Pain and happiness
Dates and dances
High school is
Nothing but change
In our hearts
Our minds
And our souls
High school is
Just another
Turning point in life

*~Julia Norris~*

# Here I am

Stuck between today and tomorrow
I have no more time to borrow
Yesterday can't be changed
And tomorrow is uncertain
But today,
Today has a thousand choices
Today I can hurt
I can heal, regret, love
I can't change yesterday
But I can decide today

# Backwards

One step forward
Two steps back
Constantly spinning
Round and round
In an endless circle
Are we making progress
Or standing still
Scared to slow down
Afraid we might realize
We are really going
Backwards . . . .

*~Julia Norris~*

# Tell Me

Tell me
Who is happier
Tell me
Who has more
The homeless man
With lint in his pockets
And love in his heart
OR
The rich man
With money in his pockets
And a cold, loveless heart
Tell me
Who is happier
Tell me
Who has more
The one
With lights in his house
Or the one
With lights in his soul
Tell me
Who is happier
Tell me
Who has more

# *Time To*

*Lost too much time*
*Too many tears*
*Time to stop*
*Move on*
*Forgive*
*And*
*Love again*
*Time to live*
*Smile and*
*Laugh*
*Time to joke*
*Be myself,*
*Let go*
*Time to go*

*~Julia Norris~*

# Today, Tomorrow, and the Past

Today
Should be the best day
Today
Should be worry free
Today
Is all we have
Today
Is what matters most

Past
Pain should not hurt you
Past
Hatred should not destroy you
Past
Troubles should not stress you
Past
Mistakes should not be dwelled on

Tomorrow
Should not worry you
Tomorrow
Should be filled with hope
Tomorrow
Should not be full of dread
Tomorrow . . . .
Tomorrow will soon be today

# Today

Tomorrow is never promised
And yesterday, we can not change
But today
Today is in our hands
Today we have the power
To change, to be happy
And most importantly,
To LOVE

*~Julia Norris~*

# Today 2

The scars of yesterday
Make us strong today
Thoughts of tomorrow
Make today seem better
But the love you show today
Makes everything better
Forever

# Today 3

If today pains you
Think of tomorrow
If tomorrow worries you
Think of yesterday
If yesterday hurts you
Think of someone you love

*~Julia Norris~*

# Each Day

Each day
Is a tomorrow,
Today, and a past
Each day
Live as your last
Each day
Wonder
Each day
Take a stand
Each day
Refuse to hate
Each day
Deny your grudge
Each day
Live your dreams
But MOST importantly
Each day
LOVE

# Empty Heart

An empty heart
Leads
To an empty soul
A loving heart
Leads
To a vibrant soul
A greedy man
Gives money
A great man
Gives love

*~Julia Norris~*

# Hopeless Lover

Painted on smiles
Dried up tears
Fake laughter
Upon my face

that's all that's left
Since you left

You were my world
My heart
And my only hope
That love was more
Than just a myth
Just a dream
Of hopeless lovers

I fell in your arms
Thinking it was safe
Never thought twice
About putting my heart
On the line
But I guess I was wrong
We all are sometimes
But
Painted on smiles
Dried up tears
And fake laughter
Is all that's left
Of this
Hopeless lover

# Empty Shell

An empty shell
Is all that remains
Of the person
You left behind
Too much pain
For one heart to take
So it left
And now
All that I am
Is an empty shell

*~Julia Norris~*

# This Pain

This pain is
Worse than any
Though it leaves
No physical scars
Only inward bleeding
And breaks
In the heart

This pain
Shows itself
In sleepless nights
And rivers of tears
Flowing down
A saddened face

This pain
Is much to great
To bear alone
Won't you bear it with me?

# Fool's Gold

Fool's gold
That's all you were
You ran away with my heart
Saw you shining
By the road
Picked you up
But little did I know

Fool's gold
That's all you were
Fool's gold
You ran away with my heart
The pain I'm feeling
Is all my fault
Cause I picked up

Fool's gold
That's all you were
Fool's gold
You ran away
With my heart
Fool's gold

*~Julia Norris~*

# Always, Forever, Never

Always
Waiting for you
Forever
Loving you
Never
Hating you
Always
Thinking of you
Forever
My heart is yours
Never
Believing you're really gone

# *Nothing But A Memory*

Memories of us
Roll through my head
As I lay here
In my bed

You left me so empty
Left me so cold
The only thing left
Is a memory
Of you and me

So broken hearted
My soul has departed
Nothing left of
Who I used to be
Nothing left
Of you and me
Nothing but a memory

*~Julia Norris~*

# Help

Pain coursing through my heart
Tears flowing from my eyes
Betrayal cutting me
Like a knife
Slicing my soul
Tearing up my spirit
Drowning in my sorrow
Not caring for tomorrow
Feeling my life
Start to fall apart

# *Never*

Mistakes you made
Too many mistakes
Irreplaceable trust
You broke
Too much pain
You caused my heart

Chances I gave you
Forgive you I did
Pain you caused
Broke my heart
Listen you never did
Love you never
Never really gave me
Trust I never should have
Never given you
Love was just a game to you
And now the mistakes you made
Have broken my heart

*~Julia Norris~*

# *So Much*

So much taken
Nothing given
Am I living
Or just breathing
So much pain
Nothing to gain
Am I losing
Am I winning
So much sorrow
Nothing for tomorrow
Am I weeping
Or just sleeping

# Does Anybody Care

*Feeling so alone*
*Memories killing me*
*My tears are drowning me*
*And I scream*
*Is anybody listening*
*Does anybody care*
*Am I wasting my time*
*Taking this breath of air*
*Nothing seems to take*
*The pain of this heartache*
*Away from me*
*I'm all alone*
*Just me and my dreams*
*Deep down inside*
*I'm breaking apart*
*Down inside*
*My broken heart*
*The pain is ripping me apart*
*And I scream*
*Is anybody listening*
*Does anybody care*
*Am I wasting my time*
*Taking this breath of air*

*~Julia Norris~*

# *Realization*

What do you do
When you know there's a problem
But not what it is
What do you do
When the answer is hidden
Behind all the little things
What do you do
To fix something unseen
What do you do
When you look in the mirror
And realize
The problem is you

# What's Keeping Me

What's keeping me
Chained to my heartache
Why am I
Imprisoned by my pain
Why do I
Still love you
You've given me
Every reason to leave
But I can't
What's got me
Locked and lost
In your hateful love
Why can't I
Let you go
What's holding me
To these shackles
I once adored
This love
I once
Would've died for
If I knew
I'd lose these chains
Walk away
From these shackles
If I could only
Find the key
To what's holding me
To your painful love

*~Julia Norris~*

# No More

No more
Room to break
But I keep on breaking
No more
Pain to take
But I keep on taking
No more
Tears to cry
But I keep on crying
No more
Life to live
But I keep on living
No more
Time to hurt
But I keep on hurting
No more
No more

# Ran Away

Cold in your heart
Lying in your eyes
False love in your arms
I fell in love
But you didn't catch me
So hard I fell
That it broke my heart
And it tore me all apart
Now I lay
Broken and confused
All because you ran away
Ran way
Scared of what you felt
Now I feel
The blood from my broken heart
And the tears from my burning eyes
Rolling in a pool
Of what's left of us
Nothing much
But the dust
From when you ran away

*~Julia Norris~*

# Day By Day

In the cold
And lonely night
I tell myself
I will be all right
But the truth is
I don't know
All I can do
Is take it
Day by day
I try not
To worry
About tomorrow
Or think of yesterday
Because it will only
Bring me more pain
So I just take it
Day by day
I just take it
Day by day

# How Much

How much
Should I forgive
How much
Should I overlook
How much
Should I forget
Before I walk away
Before I
Refuse to stay
How long
Should I give you
To change
How far
Should I go
To get you
To understand
I can only take so much
How long
Before I'm gone

*~Julia Norris~*

# Goodbye

Don't come back
Telling me your sorry
That you won't do it again
That you really love me
And how much you miss me
I've heard it all before
I've forgiven and forgotten
So much my heart is sore
There is only so much
One heart can take
And I've reached my limit
So goodbye heartache
Goodbye headache
Tired of your lies
You won't find love
In these eyes

The pain you gave me
Was more
Than the love you showed me
So goodbye heartache
Goodbye headache
Goodbye

# What's The Point

*Every time you say*
*I love you*
*You turn around*
*And hurt me*
*Every time I say*
*I trust you*
*You stab me*
*In the back*
*So what's the point*
*What's the use*
*You keep taking my heart*
*And breaking it*
*Into a million*
*Little pieces*
*So what's the point*
*What's the use*
*In even trying*
*Anymore*

*~Julia Norris~*

# *Tired*

Tired of this endless fight
Tired of the endless night
Can't take what's wrong
And make it right
None of these fights
Make anything right
We just grow
Further apart
And every word
Cuts at our heart

Am I yelling at him
Or at myself
Is he paying
For my mistakes
Should I walk away
Before I cause
Too much pain

# Free

Finally free
Free of the chains
You placed on me
Free of the heartache
Free of the pain
I've shed my last tear
Over you
Free of the hurt
Free from your memory
I've moved on
I'm free
The shackles
Of my broken heart
Have been released
My heart is free
Finally I am free

*~Julia Norris~*

# One Big Mess

You left me
With a broken heart
You left me
With shattered dreams
When you left
You ripped me up
And I started coming apart
At the seams
You're gone
And it doesn't seem real
The amount of pain I feel
Too much for me to take
Despair, bleeding from my heart
Tears, flowing from my eyes
You left me
In a mess
You left me
In one big mess

# I Cant Take

I love you
But I can't take
Another round
Of the pain
Another break
In my heart
Another rain
Of my tears
Another betrayal
Of my trust
I love you
But I can't take
The hurt you inflict
The salt you add
To old wounds
I love you
But I can't take
You leaving again

*~Julia Norris~*

# *Went Away*

I went looking
For a king
I found a joker
I gave him
All of my heart
He tore it apart
I gave him
My world
He turned it
Upside down
I gave him
My only love
He threw it away
I almost gave him
My whole life
But he just
Went away

# How Many

How many dreams
Must be broken
Before one comes true
How many times
Must a heart
Be torn in two
Before you find
True love
How many days
Have to go by
Before I forget
About you
How many tears
Must I cry
Before the pain
Finally fades away
How many?
How many?

*~Julia Norris~*

# It Doesn't Matter

*The pain*
*I feel inside*
*Is tearing me apart*
*And breaking up my heart*
*But it doesn't matter*
*Cause he isn't here*
*My only world*
*My only hope*
*My only heart*
*The only time*
*I felt alive*
*Was with him*
*And now he's gone*
*I'm dead without him*
*I don't feel a thing*
*Just a quiet observer*
*Of a breaking heart*
*Watching the tears fall*
*From an empty shell*
*Watching what used to be me*
*Start falling apart*
*But*
*It doesn't matter*
*Cause he isn't here*

# At The End Of Love

At the end of
The road of love
Tears replace kisses
Pain replaces bliss
Happiness turns to loneliness
The heat of the night turns cold
And all that's left
Is a broken heart
Dreams turn to memories
Light turns to dark
At the end of
The road of love
Sun turns to rain
Blue skies to grey
And all that's left
Is a broken lonely heart

*~Julia Norris~*

# What Do You Do?

What do you do
When you lose your everything
When your world falls apart
When someone breaks your heart
When you fall down
And no one's around
To help you back up
What do you do
What do you do then

Should you start all over
Or should you try again
Someone help me please
I'm lost
Inside my broken heart

# *Jealousy*

What's that green monster
Peeking around the corner
Every time
His phone rings
Every time
A girl looks his way
What's that green monster
Crawling into my mind
Breaking up my thoughts
Making me doubt
Things I was sure of
What's that green monster
Driving me insane
Breaking up
Everything we
Worked so hard to get?

*~Julia Norris~*

# Endless Circle

Wake up
Sorry for the fight
I love you
And a kiss goodbye
Call from work
How are you and I miss you
Walk through the door
WHAT TOOK SO LONG?
Argue fight
To hell with you GOOD NIGHT!
Wake up
Sorry for the fight
An endless circle
Of love and hate
Where does it end?
Where does it begin?
How do you stop it?

# No Resolution

*Late night*
*Details of*
*Our latest fight*
*Pour onto the pages*
*In front of me*
*Meaningless words*
*Trying to describe*
*The pain I feel*
*All these lines*
*All these words*
*And still*
*No resolution*

*~Julia Norris~*

# Perfect Imperfection

Love is
The perfect example
Of perfect imperfection
It messes everything up
And yet
We still crave it
Love drives us crazy,
Makes us angry
But we still search for it
It hurts us
Breaks, burns,
And confuses us
We are like children
Chasing a bumble bee
We get stung
But we still try
To grab it
Love is
The craziest,
Most sane thing
We'll ever want

# The Heart

So easy to deceive
So easy to break
And yet
We continue to place it
All on the line
Hoping to find
That one love
That can patch up
All the pain and sorrow
Suffered from false lovers

But it's better
To love with no fear
Of the pain that might come
Than to run and hide
Behind a wall
Missing all the joys
Of true love

*~Julia Norris~*

# Hear What I Can't Say

Listen to my heart
Hear what my lips
Dare not say
Strain your ears
Do you hear
The sound of my soul
Screaming for you

Fear of rejection
Drowns out my heart
My head fills
With reminders of
Lost loves and past pains
While my heart
Fills with a secret love
Both are going to explode

So please
Hear my heart beating
Hear what I'm not saying
Make sense of what
I can not
And hear what I
Have not the courage to say

# Hear Me Out

Listen to me
Talk to me
I know she hurt you
So long ago
But you know
I won't
Play that game
I know you want to be
Alone with your pain
But baby
Open up your eyes
And leave
The past behind
Don't you know
I LOVE YOU!

*~Julia Norris~*

# *Wish I knew*

I wish I knew
How to love you
But all I ever
Learned to do
Was scream and argue
No one showed me
How to love
Only to push and shove

I just want you to know
I want to love you
But
It'll be and uphill climb
And it'll take some time
Before I learn to love you
Like you love me

# Loving You Is Involuntary

Try and try
And
Try again
But it keeps
Getting harder
Fail and fail and
Fail again
But the attraction
Keeps getting stronger
Break and break and
Break my heart
But I can't quit
Loving you

*~Julia Norris~*

# No One Could Replace

No one could replace
The way your kisses taste
The way you make me feel
The way my heart smiles
Whenever you're around
The way I think about you
All the time
No one could replace
Your arms around me
The way I want you
Need you
Love you
No one could replace
You

# Do You

When you're alone
Do you think of me
When you're scared
Do you reach for me
When you're asleep
Do you dream of me
When you're away
Do you miss me
When you're breathing
Do you love me?

*~Julia Norris~*

# How I Know

When I sleep
I dream of you
When I smile
It's because of you
When you're away
I miss you
When you're near
I want you closer
I can't stay mad at you
I can't think of me
Without you
You are my heart
Not just a part
You are my soul
My dreams
Everything I want
And all I'll ever need

# Will You Be

Will you be
My light
In the dark
The healer of
My broken heart
Will you be
My umbrella
In the rain
The comfort
For my pain
Will you be
My love
My life
My world
Will you be
Just be
With me?

*~Julia Norris~*

# *Always Waiting*

Sitting here alone tonight
Thinking 'bout our last fight
You screamed at me
I yelled at you
Tell me baby
What good did it do?
Now you're out drinking
And I'm here thinking
It happens every time
You'll come back
Later tonight
And I'll still be here
Because you know
I love you
And I always will
So when you cool down
From our heated fight
Just come on back
And you'll find me
Waiting
Always waiting

# Love's Game

Love's game
Doesn't have any rules
Love's game
Is a tiger
That can not be tamed
It's a feeling
That can not be named
Love's game
Is something inside
That makes you feel alive
Love's game
Can not be explained
Love's game
Has a lot of fakers,
Players, dreamers,
And unlucky fools
Love's game
Will tear you apart
And break up your heart
But keeps you coming
Back for more
It's all just a part
Of love's game

*~Julia Norris~*

# Enemies Of Love

Love has many memories
Lets start with jealousy
It's starts with a doubt
That turns into a fear
Then grows into an argument
That eventually breaks up the love

Next there's gossip
He said, she said
You were doing this
Or I was doing that
And again . . . .
Doubt, fear, argue and bam
The love is gone

Love has on true friend
Trust
Trust can break up
The doubt and the fear
Before it turns into an argument
That breaks up the love

# *Love Is*

*Love is*
*The little things*
*Calling just to say*
*I love you*
*Love is*
*The kiss good night*
*The pain of parting*
*Even for a moment*
*Love is*
*The laughter we share*
*The tears you dry*
*The pain you heal*
*Love is*
*Missing you*
*Wanting you*
*Needing you*
*Love is*
*Wrapped in your arms*
*Laying beside you*
*Leaning on your shoulder*
*Love is*
*You and Me*

*~Julia Norris~*

# Love Is Bipolar

Love is a worry
A pain and a tear

Love is a blessing
A joy and a smile

Love is two-faced

But loneliness is always
Cold and dark

# Love

Love
A pain
A scar
A memory

Love
A tear
A heartache
A headache
A hurt like no other

Love
The only feeling
Worth the pain

*~Julia Norris~*

# Love is love

Love can make you hurt
Love can make you cry
It can break your heart
Tear you apart
Or heal your soul
Love can
Bring you to your knees
Or make you stand tall

Love can not be conquered
Only tasted
Love can be treasured
Or it can be wasted
Love is
As great as you make it
Or as small
As you neglect it